I think the
get informa.

-Seckin Zumbul, Izmir Turkey

I am a world traveler who has read many trip guides but this one really made a difference for me. I would call it a heartfelt creation of a local guide expert instead of just a guide.

-Susy, Isla Holbox, Mexico

New to the area like me, this is a must have!

-Joe, Bloomington, USA

This is a good series that gets down to it when looking for things to do at your destination without having to read a novel for just a few ideas.

-Rachel, Monterey, USA

Good information to have to plan my trip to this destination.

-Pennie Farrell, Mexico

Great ideas for a port day.

-Mary Martin USA

Aptly titled, you won't just be a tourist after reading this book. You'll be greater than a tourist!

-Alan Warner, Grand Rapids, USA

Even though I only have three days to spend in San Miguel in an upcoming visit, I will use the author's suggestions to guide some of my time there. An easy read - with chapters named to guide me in directions I want to go.

-Robert Catapano, USA

Great insights from a local perspective! Useful information and a very good value!

-Sarah, USA

This series provides an in-depth experience through the eyes of a local. Reading these series will help you to travel the city in with confidence and it'll make your journey a unique one.

-Andrew Teoh, Ipoh, Malaysia

>TOURIST

GREATER THAN A TOURIST- GOTHENBURG SWEDEN

50 Travel Tips from a Local

Christina De Paris

Greater Than a Tourist- Gothenburg Sweden Copyright © 2018 by CZYK Publishing LLC. All Rights Reserved.

All rights reserved. No part of this book may be reproduced in any form or by any electronic or mechanical means including information storage and retrieval systems, without permission in writing from the author. The only exception is by a reviewer, who may quote short excerpts in a review.

Cover designed by: Ivana Stamenkovic
Cover Image: https://pixabay.com/en/barken-viking-small-boom-gota-river-1785142/

CZYK Publishing Since 2011.

Greater Than a Tourist
Visit our website at www.GreaterThanaTourist.com

Lock Haven, PA
All rights reserved.
ISBN: 9781724128973

>TOURIST

>TOURIST
50 TRAVEL TIPS FROM A LOCAL

BOOK DESCRIPTION

Are you excited about planning your next trip?

Do you want to try something new?

Would you like some guidance from a local?

If you answered yes to any of these questions, then this Greater Than a Tourist book is for you.

Greater Than a Tourist – Gothenburg, Sweden by Christina De Paris offers the inside scoop on Gothenburg. Most travel books tell you how to travel like a tourist. Although there is nothing wrong with that, as part of the Greater Than a Tourist series, this book will give you travel tips from someone who has lived at your next travel destination.

In these pages, you will discover advice that will help you throughout your stay. This book will not tell you exact addresses or store hours but instead will give you excitement and knowledge from a local that you may not find in other smaller print travel books.

Travel like a local. Slow down, stay in one place, and get to know the people and the culture. By the time you finish this book, you will be eager and prepared to travel to your next destination.

TABLE OF CONTENTS

BOOK DESCRIPTION
TABLE OF CONTENTS
DEDICATION
ABOUT THE AUTHOR
HOW TO USE THIS BOOK
FROM THE PUBLISHER
OUR STORY
WELCOME TO
> TOURIST
INTRODUCTION
1. Götaplatsen (Top of Avenyn)
2. Fika, As One Does
3. Haga Old Town
4. Southern Archipelago
5. Urban Greenery
6. Lookout Points
7. Slottsskogen City Park
8. Bike Friendly City
9. Fun & Games Around Korsvägen
10. Bars & Pubs
11. Röda Sten Konsthall
12. Public Transport Experience
13. Memorable Museums
14. Lilla Bommen Harbor

15. Performance Art & Shows
16. Gustav Adolf Square
17. Christmas City and Midsummer Celebrations
18. Markets & Specialty Shops
19. Cuisine
20. Fresh Fish
21. Paddan Canal Tours & Hop On – Hop Off Bus
22. Night Life (Clubs)
23. Live Music
24. Creative Tendencies
25. Linnéstan (Linné)
26. History Fix
27. Playing Sports & Activities
28. Ferry to Hisingen
29. Frihamnen
30. Harbor & Göta River Lounging
31. Feskekôrka
32. Lake Visits
33. Shopping
34. Majorna District
35. Craft Beer & Microbreweries
36. It's Raining, Could Be Pouring
37. Northern Archipelago
38. Esperantoplatsen
39. Maritime Museum & Volvo Museum
40. Fall Festivities

\>TOURIST

41. City Jubilees
42. Architecture
43. New Year's Eve
44. Marstrand
45. Long-distance Transport
46. Vasastan District
47. Nature Outside the City
48. Accommodation
49. Sporting Events
50. Magasinsgatan Area

TOP REASONS TO BOOK THIS TRIP

50 THINGS TO KNOW ABOUT PACKING LIGHT FOR TRAVEL

Packing and Planning Tips

Travel Questions

Travel Bucket List

NOTES

DEDICATION

This book is dedicated to Johannes and my Swedish family and friends who have warmly welcomed me into their country and ensured that I am always looked after. I also want to thank my international friends here for your tips and silly dinners, and my U.S entourage for keeping up with my antics.

ABOUT THE AUTHOR

Christina has thrived as a nomadic creature for most of her adult life, but after meeting her Swedish boyfriend while traveling in 2014, she decided to take root in Gothenburg and enjoy the splendor of European living. She relocated to the western city in the beginning of 2018 and has been doing a bit of this, that and the other ever since.

HOW TO USE THIS BOOK

The Greater Than a Tourist book series was written by someone who has lived in an area for over three months. The goal of this book is to help travelers either dream or experience different locations by providing opinions from a local. The author has made suggestions based on their own experiences. Please do your own research before traveling to the area in case the suggested places are unavailable.

FROM THE PUBLISHER

Traveling can be one of the most important parts of a person's life. The anticipation and memories that you have are some of the best. As a publisher of the Greater Than a Tourist book series, as well as the popular 50 Things to Know book series, we strive to help you learn about new places, spark your imagination, and inspire you. Wherever you are and whatever you do I wish you safe, fun, and inspiring travel.

Lisa Rusczyk Ed. D.
CZYK Publishing

OUR STORY

Traveling is a passion of the "Greater than a Tourist" series creator. Lisa studied abroad in college, and for their honeymoon Lisa and her husband toured Europe. During her travels to Malta, an older man tried to give her some advice based on his own experience living on the island since he was a young boy. She was not sure if she should talk to the stranger but was interested in his advice. When traveling to some places she was wary to talk to locals because she was afraid that they weren't being genuine. Through her travels, Lisa learned how much locals had to share with tourists. Lisa created the "Greater Than a Tourist" book series to help connect people with locals. A topic that locals are very passionate about sharing.

>TOURIST

WELCOME TO
> TOURIST

>TOURIST

Gothenburg
Sweden

INTRODUCTION

"A ship in harbor is safe — but that is not what ships are built for."

— John A. Shedd.

Gothenburg is widely known in Sweden for being the capital of puns and jokes, but it's also apparent that city dwellers in the coastal town make good use of their time. Whether it's taking an afternoon fika break for coffee and a cinnamon bun, sharing some laughs over freshly-brewed beer locally produced, or escaping into the blissful nature that can be found within the city limits and out into the archipelago,

Gothenburger's are an active, fun-loving bunch eager to work hard and live life. You might find that these western Swedes are somewhat more talkative than their eastern counterpart, and as such, are apt to engage in lively conversation or direct misguided tourists visiting their city if asked. There's a general concept in Sweden, however, that all natives recognize: lagom. This Swedish word translates approximately to 'just the right amount' and is used in many instances. The archetypical Swedish proverb "lagom är bäst" is about moderation and striking a healthy balance in life, which can be conceptualized in the standards of living, social benefits, and guaranteed human rights championed in the country.

Gothenburg, or Göteborg in Swedish, is the second-largest city in Sweden and the fifth largest in the Nordic countries, yet it strikes an enjoyable poise between big-city conveniences and small-town charm. Gothenburg is a compacted, walkable city and perfect for visitors who thrive on optimizing their trip by seeing the key sites and experiencing the main attractions. Major attractions and events can be found in the city center, including nature reserves and international festivals, along with a healthy selection of museums and galleries. Downtown, the streets and

>TOURIST

waterways are steeped in history and surrounded by a fusion of 17th to 19th century edifices, wooden houses, modern restaurants and store fronts. Known for its bourgeoning trade and industrial clout due to the city's advantageous location on the Göta River at the center of Scandinavia, Gothenburg boasts the largest port in the region. This infrastructure has played a crucial role in the city's development and position in world trade starting with the Swedish East India Company, which was founded in 1731.

Embracing the oceanic climate, Gothenburg weather is influenced directly by the Gulf Stream, which brings in comfortable spring and summer weather, and slightly rainy, cold winters with a chance of snow. There's a common understanding in the city that November has some of the harshest conditions with sleet and wind, so when planning your trip, consider which time allows for the spread of activities you're most interested in. The adage rings true in this coastal town that there is no bad weather, only bad clothing, so being prepared for inopportune conditions is engrained in the locals.

Gothenburg
Climate

	High	Low
January	36	28
February	37	28
March	43	31
April	52	38
May	63	46
June	68	53
July	72	57
August	71	56
September	63	50
October	53	43
November	44	36
December	39	31

GreaterThanaTourist.com

Temperatures are in Fahrenheit degrees.
Source: NOAA

>TOURIST

1. GÖTAPLATSEN (TOP OF AVENYN)

Götaplatsen is a plaza at the start of one of Gothenburg's main thoroughfares, and houses some of the city's crown jewels, such as the Gothenburg Museum of Art, City Theatre and the Concert Hall. Götaplatsen was inaugurated in 1923 and is a base for events and special occasions, with the square's central focal point being the characteristic Poseidon statue which serves as the symbol of Gothenburg.

The Gothenburg Museum of Art is a spectacle from both outside and within, displaying one of the finest art collections in Northern Europe with significant Nordic and international artwork dating back to the 15th century to present times. In 2018, the museum was awarded "Museum of the Year" from the Swedish Museums Association and Swedish International Council of Museums for its extensive and diverse art collection, the creative work process and the scientific research integrated into the production. On display are masterpieces by renowned artists and also temporary collections. The Hasselblad Center is also located at the museum and showcases world class photo exhibitions curated by Swedish and international photographers. The state-of-the-art

Hasselblad cameras have significance by originating in Gothenburg.

This would be a nice place to begin your journey in Gothenburg, as you can walk down the street and over the bridge near Bältesspännarparken and the Stora Theater, passing many shops and parks while ending up at the Lilla Bommon district and the Opera House at the harbor.

2. FIKA, AS ONE DOES

Fika is one of the first things you learn about if given a crash course in everything Swedish. Known for consuming large quantities of coffee, Swedes are a population that has successfully designated two additional opportunities outside of early morning breakfast coffee to sip on a cup of joe and nibble on savory cakes or sweet breads. Fika basically means getting together with others at a café for a chat or taking a break from class or work, all to get that caffeine rush and a bit of head space.

Some calming fika spots include Kafé Magasinet, which has a great atmosphere and quality brewed coffee. It can be tricky to find, as it is located in a bricked-in oasis off the street, Tredje Långgatan, but finding its neighboring restaurant, Tacos & Tequila, will help you find your way. Doppio, which is close to Kafé Magasinet, is a smaller, friendly café favored by locals for its superior coffee. There's no short supply of coffeehouses in Gothenburg, so if you pass by a spot that looks cozy, it's likely that they will have decent coffee, as Swedes are critical of their brewed liquids. Da Matteo has three locations in Gothenburg which lends to its success in serving great coffee.

Ahlströms Konditori is a traditional Swedish café established in 1901 and located on Korsgatan. The atmosphere is a bit more standard than other trendier spots, but they offer historical context and a large assortment of cakes, sandwiches and light lunches. If you're feeling fancy and want to fika (interchangeably used as a noun and verb) in opulence, Dorsia is a 4-star hotel with a restaurant, lounge and rooftop terrace all set in ornate décor. Someone will greet you at the door, and it's then you say you'd like to have a fika in the setting that most appeals to you and that's conducive with the weather.

3. HAGA OLD TOWN

Haga is a picturesque neighborhood renowned for its wooden houses, 19th century architecture and quaint cafes. The district was formerly a working-class residential area during in the early 1800s during a time when the industrial and trade markets were booming, though now the district has become gentrified and replaced with post-modernistic replicas to celebrate the heritage on which the area was established. An effortless stroll along the cobblestone streets will allow for visitors to take a peek inside artisan shops or pop into one of the many inviting establishments along the way.

Café Husaren is synonymous with oversized cinnamon buns legitimately the size of your face and are paramount in getting the local experience. If you're not in the mood for a bun, there is a plethora of sweets and sandwiches at your disposal, along with beverages to boot. The main walking street in the area is Haga Nygata, but it's just as pleasant to walk down some of the residential streets as well. The Skansen Kronan fortress is in the middle of Haga and not to missed.

Jacob's Café is the largest coffee shop in Haga and has antique-style furniture, with an outside terrace if the weather is right. They serve salads, sandwiches, baked potatoes, pies and homemade cakes in their welcoming joint. In December, this district transforms into a festive wonderland with candles propped up inside windows and Jultomten (Santa Claus) figurines adorning all the open nooks. It's nice to find a good spot, and maybe even drape a blanket over you while enjoying a glass of warm glögg, the mulled wine beloved by Swedes and all those who experience it.

4. SOUTHERN ARCHIPELAGO

Frequenting the archipelago is a way of life in Gothenburg, and many outings involve ferrying out to one of more than 20 islands that speckle the western coastline. The islands are characterized by smooth rock, so visitors can take in tranquil Scandinavian landscapes while trekking on nature trails or bathing in the sea. Bringing a picnic and finding a spot on the rocks is common among the locals. Some visitors will make a short trip to circumnavigate the landmass, and others make an all-day excursion out of it. There are some islands that have cafés and restaurants, providing the option for restroom stops along the way.

The car-free southern archipelago can be reached from Saltholmen terminal or Stenpiren Transport Hub where several ferries launch and transport island-goers year-round (although Stenprien has less frequent times in winter). Taking the ferry from Stenpiren will give you a more economical boat tour through the harbor and out into the open ocean. There isn't a guide explaining the sights, but it's still nice to see the city from a different perspective. Styrsö and Donsö are the largest islands and are connected by a bridge, attracting the most people to their shores.

Ferry tickets can be purchased through the Västtrafik To Go app or with the same card used for trams and buses. Västtrafik tickets last 90 minutes, so if you bought one to the ferry terminal it should also be valid for your boat ride. There are ferries via Saltholmen that will take you to some of the smaller islands such as Asperö, Brännö and others, but be sure that you go to an island for tourists and not a residential island. On Brännö during the summer there are dance parties on Saturdays that can be a lively way to spend the well-lit evenings.

If you don't have time to make it out to an island but still want to take a brisk dip into the sea, Saltholmen has some nice bathing areas.

>TOURIST

Also, be cognizant of the return ferry schedule so you don't find yourself scrambling to get back to the mainland. When in doubt, the ferry staff are happy to help in assuring passengers are informed. Generally, boats depart once every hour to the bigger islands but it's best to check timetables at the Västtrafik website to confirm routes and times align with your plans. Winter months will have fewer ferry times than summer.

5. URBAN GREENERY

Gothenburg has 2,700 hectares of green space within its domain, so it's common for locals to take a break from the bustle and surround themselves with the serenity of nature, even during a lunch break. Two of the largest and most attractive grounds in the city are Trädgårdsföreningen (The Garden Society) and the Botanical Garden. Vegetation sprouted from around the globe thrive in both locations and are meticulously labeled by their scientific name and place of origin. The flora blossoming at both locations will depend on which season you visit, with summer offering the greatest presentation.

The Garden Society is a beautiful park with open fields, plant and flower beds, and a greenhouse. It's centrally located at Bältesspännarparken, directly next to Kungsportsplatsen tram/bus stop. There is no charge to enter, and the greenhouses are a welcome delight to explore at any time of the year. A small children's park can be found near the fountain at the heart of the park, and toward the far reaches you'll enter a flourishing rose garden that's best seen in the warmer months of the year. Like many establishments, the cafés connected to the park are seasonal, meaning they'll operate roughly between April and early October.

The Botanical Garden is a short walk or tram ride, depending on where you're based in the city. If arriving by tram (Botaniska Trädgården stop), you'll just need to cross the street and walk a short distance before arriving at the entrance. There is no fee, but you can make a donation, to visit the expansive beauty the grounds behold. The gardens are grouped and demarcated, including a rock garden with a vantage point that provides an overview of the park and part of the city. You can enter the sizable Änggårdsbergen nature reserve through the Botanical Garden if you're in the market for a longer hike. Gotheburgers are a resilient bunch and can be found promenading in the forests even during the thick of winter with layers of snow or sludge packed on the ground.

6. LOOKOUT POINTS

Gothenburg is rather flat, but has some elevations throughout the city. If you're keen on getting your bearings of the layout, there are several lookout points easily accessible from within the city. The most notable one is from Skansen Kronan, a fortress from 1697 that sits at the apex of Risåsberget hill in Haga. The point offers a remarkable 365-degree view of the city and has a café in summer. Remember that due to Sweden's northernly position, days can be very long in the summer and short in the winter, so sunrises and sunsets could occur at all different times of the day depending on the month.

Masthugget Church lies slightly away from the city center, but is worth the trek to get a sweeping view of the Göta River and the Älvsborgs suspension bridge that connects the north and south sides of the city. The characteristic Nordic-style church dates back to 1914 and is located on top of a hill in Masthugget.

If you're in the mood for an upscale atmosphere while you gaze out at the city, you can order a cocktail or shrimp sandwich from the Heaven 23 restaurant and bar on the top floor of Svenska Mässan tower one. The sky bar is located right at the Korsvägen transport hub.

Guldhedstornets Café is a more economic approach than Heaven 23 to seeing the city from an elevation while also being able to grab a drink or light meal. The ambiance inside isn't necessarily as trendy as other cafés, but though still a good option if you're in the Södra Guldheden district.

7. SLOTTSSKOGEN CITY PARK

Slottsskogen is a sprawling city park that has something for everyone and is located in the middle of town at Linnéplatsen tram/bus stop. This is Gothenburg's main park and a frequent destination for locals to take a stroll, bring a picnic, or get some exercise. Locals often take advantage of the relaxed atmosphere in a mix of planned park and natural forest, and also enjoy the loads of activities available in this recreational park. If you have children, Plikta

>TOURIST

park is an all-time favorite among Gothenburgers, with a spirited architectural playground.

There is a petting zoo with pony rides that operates from April to September, and also a park zoo that is free to enter and open year-round. The zoo has enclosures for Nordic animals, such as moose, elk and seals, among other creatures. Slottsskogen also has the only public observatory in Sweden, Slottsskogsobservatoriet, where visitors gaze through a telescope into space during the darker season, mainly between September and March. If you prefer more Earthy attractions, the Natural History Museum is also located in the park and has on display the world's only mounted blue whale.

You can take easy while overlooking lush landscapes at Villa Belparc for a nice meal or fresh treats from the bakery. There's also Café Björngårdsvillan that dates back to 1906 and is located in the middle of the park, serving coffee and light meals. If you find yourself in the swing of things with extra time, try your skills putting a few rounds at the mini-golf course. Summer is an exciting season in Gothenburg and there's a steady stream of activities at Slottsskogen, one being the Way Out West music festival that attracts big international acts headlining the 3-day event. Should luck has its way, you could also enjoy the once-a-year performance by the Gothenburg Symphonic Orchestra in its free open-air concert.

8. BIKE FRIENDLY CITY

Gothenburg is an inviting city to explore by bike. It has dedicated lanes for cyclists connecting all sides of the city, along with serene pathways through tree-topped spaces. The Styr & Stall shared bike scheme allows riders to borrow and return bikes to any of the 60 locations scattered around the city, paying at the kiosk located at the rental zones. The transaction can be done in English and it's only possible to pay with a major debit or credit card.

The three-day rentals are convenient, great value for money and can be purchased from any of the terminals for 25 kronor. This card contains an ID which you will need to enter each time you borrow a bike, in addition to a PIN selected by you. It is important that you keep your ticket in the event that any issue may arise. The first half hour of every ride is always free, regardless of the number of trips per day, but you'll accrue a small charge if you go over the time limit. Make sure to activate the anti-theft device which has a built-in key if parking your bike somewhere. If there are no available stands at the station, use the terminal to locate a nearby station with availability and bikes will give you 15 minutes free of charge to get there.

Although some areas may seem daunting to maneuver through, most locals recognize cyclists have the right of way and will generally yield to them. The scenario isn't as intimidating as say in Amsterdam, however, remain vigilant when cruising through crosswalks given the extensive network of buses and trams. If you're traveling with a bike and want to get in a good distance ride, the trail from Linnéplatsen to Billdal is a beautiful trip through nature and a solid depiction of the socioeconomic stratas of the city.

9. FUN & GAMES AROUND KORSVÄGEN

You might see people walking in the streets, dwarfed by boxes of savory sweets that they've just been awarded at Liseberg, an amusement park anchored in the midst of the city the largest in Scandinavia in terms of number of rides. Here you can get slung around on a rollercoaster and get a bird's-eye view on the Ferris wheel, among many other jaunts. Known for its plentiful fair-like games, this attraction dates back to 1923 and is even popular among the locals who step foot inside and revert back to their childhood selves, pandering in friendly competition and then taking a celebratory drink or meal in one of the restaurants within the park. Although this adventure center is open year-round, some rides are seasonal. For a nominal fee, visitors can often enjoy live performances at the amphitheater or just stroll through the whimsical play town made for any aged folk if you don't feel like buying the extra tickets required to play the game and ride the rides. It's possible to buy an all-in-one admission that will include rides and game, and also there's a group rate if you have 15 people or more.

If the weather isn't cooperating, just next door sits Universium, the science center with an indoor rainforest and exhibitions built to make your mind dance and your senses heighten. At the center, nature and animals mix with innovative technology and stimulating experiments. This center is open 365 days a year, so if you end up wanting something to do on a rainy Monday, this is a decent option, especially if you're traveling with children. The World Culture

>TOURIST

Museum neighbors Universium and is housed in an award-winning building designed by renowned architects. The contents inside the structure are equally as intriguing, bringing an awareness to social contexts, contemporary art, and exciting activities. The museum is a meeting point for those who are curious about the interconnectedness of the world and crave thought-provoking entertainment. To add to the excitement, this museum is free and open every day of the week except Monday.

10. BARS & PUBS

Andra Långgatan and Tredje Långgatan are the premier avenues if you're determined to enjoy a beverage or meal in a celebrated spot. These two streets run parallel and are just a block away from each other, so it's easy to make your rounds at several bars, pub crawl style. If you're not up to mosey, many places have varying atmospheres and don't charge a cover to go in, so you can step inside, browse what's behind the bar and figure out what's your style. There are two universities based in the downtown area – University of Gothenburg and Chalmers University of

Technology – so there is a youthful vibe to the city, especially on the weekends.

Drinking can be costly in Gothenburg, so if you're trying to conserve your funds while out, Hamburger Restaurant, King's Head and nearby spots will have at least one inexpensive beer on tap and are cozy enough pubs to start at before heading to Ölstugan Tullen or Jerntorgets Brygghus to taste one of many Gothenburg-brewed craft beers or an inventive cocktail. There are oftentimes establishments that have specials, some saying "After Work" which basically means co-workers getting together for a drink.

When traveling through Gothenburg during the week and ending up on these streets in the evening, you can find some venues have trivia in English and open mic night. Skål Pub also has these activities and is about a ten-minute walk from Andra Långgatan.

11. RÖDA STEN KONSTHALL

Röda Sten is an eclectic art house with international exhibitions intriguing to the mind and soul. The hall exhibits contemporary art and performances by Swedish and international artists.

>TOURIST

There are four floors in the 1940s former boiler house that contain paintings, photography, performances, video and sound art along with opportunities to partake in creative workshops and conversations.

The namesake, Röda Sten (Red Stone), derives from a mythical stone painted in red located on the shore just west of the brick building, and when walking to it you can see many stone sculptures decorating the landscape. The marina is also home for vintage boats if you fancy a look. Draken (The Dragon) is the only legal graffiti wall in Gothenburg; you might notice that city does not have much graffiti in the streets generally. The 41-meter-long sculpture is available to anyone to paint on at any time, so if you're eager to leave your mark on the city (even if temporarily) bring what you need to express your creative side. Röda Sten doesn't sell any paint but promotes participation.

The center is located in Majorna along the river and directly under the Älvsborg Bridge. It's easy to take the 3 tram and walk a short distance toward the water to visit the gallery. There are plenty of places to sit around Röda Sten and there's also a nice restaurant and café.

12. PUBLIC TRANSPORT EXPERIENCE

The notable public transportation system reaches any space imaginable that a tourist would want to see in Gothenburg. The stops might not take you to the doorstep of your destination, but the walk to arrive wherever you're going will be reasonable. The trams, buses and ferries all operate under the same transportation network, so you can easily purchase fares through the Västtrafik To Go app and check times of the fastest and most logical routes on the Reseplaneraren app, both of which are in English. Driving a car could be avoided entirely, but if you do have one, parking can be limited and have a steep price tag.

If you don't plan to have internet access on your phone while traveling, it's best to buy a rechargeable card at either 7/11 or Pressbyrån convenient stores, in which case you must put a minimum 100 kronor. It's also possible to purchase tickets on the tram once you step aboard, however, that is not possible on the buses and ferries. The stops will all have Swedish names and be announced in Swedish, so it's wise to keep an eye on the screen in anticipation for your stop. Transportation services run around the clock but in the late evenings and early mornings they are more infrequent during. Swedes will generally choose an open row of seats instead of sitting next to someone, so embrace your personal space like the locals and take an unoccupied row when possible.

13. MEMORABLE MUSEUMS

Gothenburg museums have curated exhibitions that satisfy a variety of interests and most are located in the city center. If your trips are typically affixed to museum visits, it could be wise and economical to purchase the Gothenburg Pass: an all-in-one ticket into over 30 attraction and museums in the city. Check out the website and determine which destinations you're interested in going to and you might find that you could save a fair chunk of change. Also, if you're a student or have children under certain ages you might be entitled to a discount. Like in most major cities, Mondays the museums are closed.

The most comprehensive collections of Gothenburg history lie in The Museum of Gothenburg, since the institution was formed by the merger of several former museums. The arts gallery has furniture, archaeological finds, photography, cars, clothes and more. Overall, the vast collections contain nearly 1 million objects, 2 million images and spans over 12,000 years of history starting with the Stone Age. The museum also houses Europe's largest and most complete computer collection. There are permanent collections, but also rotating exhibitions, so browse the website to see what's on display. There is free admission for visitors under the age of 25.

The Röhsska Museum is devoted to design and art handicrafts, and opened in 1916. It's located just off the main boulevard, Avenyn, on Vasagatan street. The architectural design of the building is typical for the national romantic spirit of that time, and within its walls is a range of contemporary designs to Chinese ceramics dating back thousands of years.

14. LILLA BOMMEN HARBOR

Lilla Bommen is hub for a variety of adventures. Here, depending on one's interests, the most captivating spectacle could either be the Barken Viking, a sailing ship completed circa 1907, or the Lipstick building as it is commonly referred to as, which is a post-modern high-rise adorning the district.

>TOURIST

The ship contains a nautical-themed hotel and restaurants, and it's also possible to walk in for a drink while sitting in the main deck of the vessel.

Encompassing a marina, the area is the gateway to dinner or lunch cruises, and for the adventurous, kayak rentals. The Opera House is adjacent to Lilla Bommen. Strömma is a sightseeing tours company, excursions to Vinga to see the city's iconic lighthouse, Marstrand, Hisingen and other locations. You can choose an all-day tour, or hourly tours, some which include dinner. Check out their website to see if you can work one of the tours into your plans. If purchasing the tickets at the harbor be prepared to pay by card because they are a cashless enterprise.

15. PERFORMANCE ART & SHOWS

Culture and art are prominent features in many Gothenburgers' routines and there is a multitude of venues which offer Swedish and international performances on both small and grand scales. The Opera House is one of the architectural highpoints of the city and was inspired by the nautical and industrial character that typifies the city. There is an array of acts performed on stage at the venue, so researching what's available and prices will be the best way to see if you're spending an evening at the Opera House while in town. The performances can be ballets, plays, music acts, among other entertainment. Even if you don't plan on attending a show, merely seeing the building is a delightful experience on its own.

The Folktheater located at Järntorget aims to put on productions that are provocative, touching and entertaining, and has two stages with plays and guest performances as the traditional line up. The Gothenburg City Theatre is the oldest city theater in the country and also one of Swedens's largest dramatic stages, located at Götaplatsen. Also found off Avenyn is the Stora Teatern, which puts on shows from modern circuses and world concerts to philosophical dialogues and international dance. The 19th-century building itself is quite beautiful and sometimes hosts watch parties for major televised sports with a big screen out front.

>TOURIST

16. GUSTAV ADOLF SQUARE

This plaza dons a statue of King Gustav Adolf – who declared in that very spot that Gothenburg be built where it stands today – and is where you can experience the city in its historical glory. Formerly, Gothenburg was started on Hisingen across the river, but was subsequently burned down by the Danes in 1609. It is here that Gothenburg has some of its most enduring buildings such as Kronhuset, a mid-17th century Dutch-style former depot for military uniforms and equipment. Many of the wooden buildings originally built during the same era were burned to the ground, so as it stands many structures date back to the mid-18th century.

The City Hall and municipal building comprise the courtyard's facades and you'll find the historical area (known as Kronhusbodarna) just a short distance behind them. You won't go out of your way to get to this area, as it is located directly next to Brunnsparken and can be taken as an alternative route to get to the harbor where the Viking ship and Opera are located.

Kronhusbodarna also functions as a living artisanal mecca in an archaic setting with elder Swedes selling sweets, leather goods, soaps and a number of market items that are authentic and somewhat more reasonably priced than you'll find in Haga. The Christmas market is a favorite for locals wanting to find high-quality craftmanship and to support local small businesses.

Just next to Gustav Adolf Square are steps that lead down to the canal, flanked with large bronze lion statues (Lejontrappan), and attracts many locals to take a break from the grind and admire the surrounding cityscape.

17. CHRISTMAS CITY AND MIDSUMMER CELEBRATIONS

The city of Gothenburg from mid-November to December is a Christmas wonderland. If you're here during the fall and winter, you'll notice the days are rather short, lending the night as a time to shine for twinkling lights. Candles will illuminate windows everywhere, and in the city center, the thoroughfare from Lilla Bommen harbor area to Liseberg Amusement Park will be ornamented with a canopy of lights. The festive atmosphere will emanate from the facades, landscapes and store fronts, and it's possible that snowfall could blanket the open spaces, although it's not guaranteed. In Sweden, Christmas celebrations are celebrated with family and friends on the 24th of December, and Swedes have certain delicacies as the holiday's staple such as: herring, meatballs, ham, potatoes, gravlax (cured salmon), glögg and schnapps, rice porridge, among other things. If you're fortunate enough to share Christmas with some Swedes, then you'll get to listen to the jolly schnapps songs they fondly recite periodically throughout the dinner.

Earlier in the year, if you've planned your trip over the equally (if not more) beloved holiday of Midsummer's Eve, then you could witness some seemingly peculiar activity that is a naturally occurring rite in Swedish culture, such as raising and dancing around a large, flowered maypole and hopping around like frogs to charming tune. This day in June usually is celebrated on Midsummer's Eve and marks the longest day of the year (summer solstice), so many Swedes and adopted locals will party into late hours with ample daylight shining on their smiling faces. This occasion too calls for designated schnapps shots and songs, along with similar food to Christmas but plus eggs and knäckebröd and minus gravlax and rice porridge.

Many people will retreat to the countryside for Midsummer celebrations at a summer cottage, so you could find parts of the city a bit quiet during that weekend in June.

18. MARKETS & SPECIALTY SHOPS

To get a general idea of what kind of consumable goods and hand crafts are available in Gothenburg, take a walk through Saluhallan at Kungsportplatsen. This is the biggest indoor market in town and has spices, coffee, cheese, fruit and other delicacies from around the globe. Saluhallen, or The Market Hall, has around forty shops and places to eat, and stays open until 6:00 p.m. most days, except Sunday when it is closed.

Saluhallan is more of a set-price kind of place, so if you're a master bargainer, try your haggling skills (or just pay full price) at Kvibergs Market. Located not far from the city center is the largest market in Gothenburg. The market's eclectic, multicultural and animated atmosphere is great way interact with the locals and make some economical purchases. Every weekend there are more than 200 sellers in stalls and under tents selling foods, attire, knickknacks, and

>TOURIST

more, and also people who repair items and vend grub from food trucks.

Not in the mood for that kind of stimulation overload? Hung-Loi Market and Gain Trading Asien Livs are Asian food markets in the city .that have products spanning from the entire Eastern hemisphere have massive sections of authentic ramen if you're budget needs reconfiguring. If you want to embrace your Swedish atmosphere and have a sweet tooth, you can take part in a national tradition of getting candies on Saturday. Children grow up anticipating this weekend day because it signifies getting goodies (godis means candy in Swedish).

There are lots of candy shops in town, but one of the largest ones is down the road from Gain Trading Asien Livs, walking toward the sailing boat in the harbor, called 4-Gott. There are actually a few locations of this candy store in the city, which is also a great place to get inexpensive Swedish souvenirs to bring back from your trip. In the trendier, upscale districts the souvenirs will be better quality, but more expensive. Buying a red Dala Horse as a souvenir is one of the most quintessential Swedish gifts, a beloved symbol of the nation, and can be found at 4-Gott.

19. CUISINE

Gothenburg is a town of foodies and a multicultural fusion of cuisines due it's incredible diversity. There is an abundance of restaurants to choose from, which can be overwhelming for diners, but the streets with the highest concentration of popular eateries includes: Linnégatan, Andra Långgatan, Tredje Långgatan, and along Avenyn. Eating out is a costly activity in Sweden, so it's wise to split your meal times between a sit-down restaurant and a food stand, such as those that serve korv (sausage) or kebab, both commonly eaten food locally.

Gothenburgers will explain that when they go out to eat, they don't usually eat Swedish food, as they will eat typical dishes at home, with family or perhaps in cafeterias at work or university. As a tourist, however, having an authentic Swedish dinner at a local's home most likely won't be in the cards, in which case you can visit Café Du Nord. Swedes take pride in their quality meatballs, a specialty at this establishment, which dates back to 1875. Hamburgers are also a heavy favorite in town and you'll find most places outside of vegetarian/vegan restaurants serve them. Tugg is a burger spot that stays busy due to

>TOURIST

their high-quality meat and fresh ambiance. Gothenburg has a booming vegan scene, with Kafé Frilagret having many options with a frequented Saturday brunch, and Blackbird, a cooperative restaurant run by vegans located in the trendy Majorna district being two of them. Café Andrum is a solid vegetarian restaurant centrally located near Gustav Adolf Square.

Rest assured that many restaurants consider patrons' dietary preferences and will have gluten-free, vegan and vegetarian options. International influences shape a lot of Gothenburger's diets, and if you're craving another type of exotic food, you can visit Moon Thai Kitchen and transport yourself while dining in tuk-tuks. Sushi spots run abound in the city, some well-liked one being Washabi, Haiku and Super Sushi. If you're ready to drop a hefty amount on a dinner and want an upscale experience, Gothenburg has six Michelin restaurants serving a spread of Swedish and international dishes prepared by top-class chefs.

20. FRESH FISH

Gothenburg is a magnet for consumers of fish, as one of its flourishing industries is fueled by its proximity to the ocean. Catches are brought in from the harbor and make their way dining tables the same day, so if you're craving fresh fish then you'll enjoy eating at one of the many establishments in Gothenburg. For seafood fanatics, Fiskekrogen prepares a plethora of sea creatures in both classic and innovative cooking techniques. This restaurant has a buffet if you want to go all out, and ranges in price depending on the kind of seafood you want to eat. Although this spot could run up a hefty bill, with the quality of food and bottomless plate factored in, you could see it as an incredible deal. Children between 7 and 13 years old eat for half the price.

At Fiskhamn, there is a fish auction held early in the mornings from Monday to Friday where wholesale buyers can bid on the hauls brought in from Sweden, Norway and Denmark. Private persons can't buy any of the fish, but it's still a unique experience to witness if the industry intrigues you enough. There are also training courses you can look into on the Gothenburg fish auction website. Don't fret about not being able to buy fish at the fish auction, because you can purchase seafood from one of the grocery stores (Hemköp or ICA to name two) in the city, or from a fish truck sometimes parked outside the food marts.

21. PADDAN CANAL TOURS & HOP ON – HOP OFF BUS

To get a comprehensive overview of the city and its history, step aboard the Paddan Sightseeing boats which launch from the city center at Kungsportsplatsen. The tours have been operating since 1939 and last 50 minutes; you can see the old moat and canals dating from the 17th century while learning about the history of Gothenburg's construction and defense. The lively guide on board will inform you about the city's history, current happenings, and sights along the route, combining stories, quips, and anecdotes which make for great entertainment. It's also a great way to watch the locals in their natural habitat hanging out along the canals.

The company's website will list all prices and details about the trip, along with available dates. The tours typically operate from March to October. It's also possible to purchase a 24-hour Paddan hop-on/hop-off tour and roam as you please at specific stops such as: Kungsportsplatsen, Lejontrappan, Lilla Bommen and Feskekôrka.

If you enjoy sightseeing by bus, there's a double-decker Hop On – Hop Off Bus that allows tourists to utilize their 24-hour pass to explore seven of the most popular spots in town. The tour takes an hour if you don't disembark from the bus, and it's also possible to combine the bus and boat tours. There are headsets that will deliver the tour in eight languages and a covering on the top deck should the rain pick up. Note that bus tours don't operate from November to late March.

22. NIGHT LIFE (CLUBS)

Most Swedes are revelers both abroad and locally, so it's no surprise that the nightlife in Gothenburg is kinetic and varied. Many venues have several levels and dance floors with music booming and an energy that travels through the space. Avenyn has the highest concentration of clubs in the city, with Park Lane, Excet, Lounges, and Yaki-da serving as some of the most popular haunts. Port du Soleil is a summer club with a Mediterranean vibe and excites with its exotic motifs and live musical performances. Most clubs charge a cover fee ranging between 100 to 250 kronor, so if you're committed to having that dance party atmosphere, be prepared to pay the price. Some clubs also have age restrictions and nights dedicated to either a teenage crowd and clubgoers that are 23 to 25, and up.

Yaki-da is a well-liked hang for its multistory dance floors, but also because on Wednesdays from 7 – 10 p.m the club serves free pizza and has ping pong. Drinks are half price during happy hour and there is also a restaurant in case you missed the free food. Gretas is the oldest LGBT club in Gothenburg, and Bee Kök & Bar is another locale that celebrates the gay community, but it's not unusual for there to be hetero partiers as well. If you're looking to embark on the night with some pre-drinking involved, find your closest Systembolaget – the government-owned liquor store – and you might find yourself acting like a kid in a candy shop given its overly sufficient inventory. Hoki Moki and Nefertiti Jazz Club are both great options if you're looking to listen to local artists and versatile music sets. They also do well in promoting female musical acts and DJs and have various bars and dance floors to explore.

23. LIVE MUSIC

Gothenburger's love music and gravitate toward it for many occasions. Whether it be live performances at a venue or a party that's blasting an attuned playlist on Spotify – a company created by Swedes and headquartered in Stockholm – music is constant source of engagement in Sweden. Gothenburg keeps a pretty active line up of international artists and national treasures on the docket, along with many, many people you've never heard of but still could very well enjoy listening to.

Nefertiti Jazz Club has a stable roster of artists playing jazz, folk, soul, rock, and other genres of music on stage from between 40 to a few hundred kronor. On Saturdays, they hit the DJ world beats when the venue becomes a dance club. Sticky Fingers is the premier rock club in Gothenburg, while Studio HPKSM has a consistent spread of sounds across the spectrum, all listed on their website. Liseberg Amusement Park also has a main stage that hosts crowd-pleasing musical acts from Sweden and sometimes international names as well. Performances are included in the general admission to the park. Yaki-da and Trädgår'n are offer a dose of spinning DJs and all out bands.

Musikens Hus is a location where people can enjoy entertainment free of charge; this venue is located in the trendy Majorna district and extends a substantial cultural scene in the city. The city's major stadiums, Ullevi, Gamla Ullevi, and Scandinavium, frequently book musical acts from across the globe that come to Gothenburg and medicate music fiends with a dose of live melodies. The city's tourism website (Goteborg.com) will have a complete run down of shows up to a year in advance.

24. CREATIVE TENDENCIES

Many Gothenburger's have a deep appreciation for the arts, demonstrated by the decorative store fronts, array of galleries and performance halls. Many creative minds come together to expose their craft in the form of festivals, restaurants, musical sets and dramatic recitals. Lagerhuset contains the city's Literature House and hosts a literary reading that's free and open to the public, called Spittoon. The event's Facebook page is the best way to get information about dates, but the readings are usually the last Thursday evening of the month. Individuals from around the globe, speaking a variety of languages, gather and share their writings with a warm audience. It's possible to present a short story, poetry or other literary works on stage if you contact the organizers a week or even days ahead of the monthly event.

Singing is another creative expression that can be unabashedly practiced in some of the pubs through karaoke nights. Haket and Skål Pub are two public places to have a good time and sing your favorite show tunes. Skål Pub also has an open mic night if you're looking for a medium to entertain more conventionally. Sing Sing is a Vietnamese kitchen that takes a different approach to karaoke by renting out rooms to groups to get silly on a more private level.

Konstepidemin is Sweden's biggest workplace for independent artists and assembles players in the arts and culture of Gothenburg, spurring ideas and thoughts in visual arts, literature, theater and music. The creative venue (near Linnéplatsen bus/tram stop) has both studios people rent, exhibition halls, and workshops offered by the talented individuals who are accepted into the collective. You can inquire through the Konstepidemin website about workshops even though there might not be any listed.

>TOURIST

25. LINNÉSTAN (LINNÉ)

Linnéstan, commonly known as Linné, is a laid-back district with local charm and a variety of independent shops, cafés, eateries and bars. One of the hallmarks of the neighborhood along the main street is Hagabion and Bar Kino, a combined movie theatre, restaurant and bar. In the summer, the area out front is transformed into a societal outdoor eating space, just as many establishments offer during the warmth and extended daylight.

Oscar Fredriks church is a beautiful Neo-Gothic style place of worship that can be seen from the street running directly next to Hagabion and is truly breathtaking. It's best seen from this location, and on clear days, during the morning and afternoon when it's illuminated by the sunshine. Along the main tree-lined boulevard, are tall stone buildings, many from the beginning of the 20th century alongside other Post-Modern houses from the 1980s. Sjutton Kvadratmeter Lakrits (a small shop with a black and white awning) has licorice in different flavors and from different parts of the world. Swedes grow up eating salty black licorice that's distinct and worth experiencing.

26. HISTORY FIX

Should you find yourself in need of century-old European history, a few places lie a short distance from the city center. Tjolöholm castle was built between 1898-1904 and tickets can be bought on location or on their website for a guided viewing (the only way to see the castle from inside). The 45-minute tour consists of a trip through one of the most complete 18th-century estates in Scandinavia and is in Swedish unless otherwise listed on their website; however, pamphlets with room descriptions are available in English, German and French. The predominantly in Tudor-style castle is Sweden's leading Arts and Crafts property. The estate's garden is open all year round and does not require an entrance fee. The nearest public transport stop is Torpa Smedja, which is roughly four-kilometers from the castle, so take consideration when planning a visit.

Jonsered Gardens, or Jonsereds Trädgårdar, avowals a heritage stretching back to the 1800s. The mansion built on the premise was completed in 1868 and its vast garden is comprised of four individual plots separated by theme. The history of the space is rich, starting out as a well-manicured garden with

>TOURIST

vegetable crops at the public's disposal, to a faded memory after factories closures, to a revitalized site in 2014 of organic growing and social responsibility.

Gunnebo House neoclassical-style mansion is one of Sweden's most complete 18th-century estates. The house is set up as a museum recreating the 18th-century and one of the finest and best-preserved baroque gardens in the country. To see the interior, you must book a guided tour, however, the garden is open to visitors. The estate is in Mölndal, just south of the Gothenburg. All three locations have places to get refreshments and offer generous opening hours and days considering many places are closed during the winter in Sweden.

27. PLAYING SPORTS & ACTIVITIES

Exercise and routines don't always fit into the equation while traveling, so having a fun alternative could be a way for you to get the circulation pumping. Gothenburg is site to the world's largest sand volleyball hall with 16 courses indoors, and has a unique tropical environment that makes you think you're at white sand beach on a remote island. Beach Center, which is located in Kviberg, has music sounding over the speakers for players to get into their groove, and there's a restaurant and bar to quench any hunger or thirst that could be lingering. The fee is minimal to rent a court and slots can be booked online.

Maybe you're one for individual sports or leisurely activity, so you might like to visit Valhallabadet, the public swimming pool directly in town. Since 1956, the facility has preserved its contemporary style and is proud to be one of Scandinavia's largest indoor swimming pools. The tiled mosaics that adorn the walls of the pool hall are elaborate and vibrant. The water could be slightly cooler than you're used to, but what's comforting is that there's a steamy sauna that awaits. There's a small entrance fee which includes

>TOURIST

access to changing rooms and the facilities on site. Rules posted in Swedish and accompanied by photos are generally posted, but there's no harm in asking what protocol is at the facility. There are also a number of golf courses and ranges nearby that are mostly seasonal and are open to the public.

Directly next to Beach Center is the Priority Serneke Arena, which has seven floors of sports, ranging from cross-country skiing to handball and football (soccer) that you can rent. The arena is unique in that is offers a skiing facility indoors with a 1.2-kilometer-long ski track. There are two classic tracks and one skate track, and if you opted to leave your skis at home, you can rent some as well as clothing at Intersport ski-rental. To get to Kviberg, you can take the 6, 7, or 11 trams or bus 58 or 519 to Brovägen, and then it's a short walk to the complex. Golf is played seasonally by some in the city, and two clubs with challenging courses and driving ranges are Sisjö Golf and Göteborgs Golf Klubb which are open to the public.

28. FERRY TO HISINGEN

Hisingen is the island north of the city and has grown exponentially in the past decades. Now, waterfront apartments and a developing university campus and social scene are enticing many to consider crossing the river to settle down in districts that have been transformed from areas where old shipyards and industrial buildings used to be the only development. It's possible to spend a few hours exploring some of the major districts such as Lindholmen, Eriksberg and Frihamnen. There is a ferry from Stenpiren to Lindholmen that is free and can be identified by waving "Gratis" flags.

Lindholmen is situated between Eriksberg and Frihamnen and all three are within a walkable distance from one another. Lindholmen is home to one of the Chalmers University campuses and features some of the more fascinating modern structures in the city. One is a multicolored, slanting cylindrical building called Kuggen (the cog), which can be seen from where the ferry docks. Outdoor spaces and boardwalks along the water make the area a nice atmosphere and break from the movement of the city center. If you're keen on taking a more vertical hike, you can ascend the trails on Ramberget

>TOURIST

mountain in Keiller's Park and observe the archipelago, industrial district and shipyards. Notably a steep climb, the park is a mix of landscape greenery and natural forest.

Formerly the location for one of the largest employers in Gothenburg, the shipbuilding industries gradually liquidated. However, the city has been praised for successfully developing the areas into vibrant residential spaces. Eriksberg can be localized by the iconic orange-red crane towering above the town's edge, associated with this bygone industrial era. This is another emerging city that has attractive parks, a boardwalk along with water, and some restaurants, and ice cream shops. Explore a replica of the East Indiaman Götheborg that sank outside Gothenburg upon the return from China in 1745. The East Indiaman Götheborg is a genuine working ship with a rich history. This 18th-century style ship was built in modern times but by archaic construction methods and represents the influential trade industry that once helped elevate the city's status in the world. Since the ship's maiden voyage to China from 2005 to 2007, the ship has executed a total of nine expeditions around the world. A guided tour is about an hour, just be sure to check prices and times on their website.

29. FRIHAMNEN

Frihamnen on Hisingen has become more developed with not necessarily much to see in terms on buildings and restaurants, but there is a free public pool called Pöl Harbour and sauna located directly on the harbor's edge that offers a unique experience to swim in purified water pumped from six meters below the surface of the river. It takes on an identity as an infinity pool but more at a grassroots level than lap of luxury. There is also a small, cooler dip that's filled with saltwater and purified after being pumped in from the brackish river. There is a restaurant on site where you can enjoy food and drinks but it's prohibited to bring any refreshments out to the recreational areas. An interesting component to the park is a changing area constructed from 12,000 recycled glass bottles. The sauna is an abstract structure that can be frequented at your leisure during the warmer months and then reserved during the winter. The pool is closed from October to March.

Jubileumsparken (Jubileum Park) is part of the Gothenburg 400th anniversary celebration, and a place that brings the city closer to the water. The park will continue to evolve and change beyond the city's anniversary in 2021. It already has a wooden

>TOURIST

playground, skate park and the first and only outdoor roller derby rink. The plan is for it to expand as a public meeting place.

There's a bus that arrives directly in front of the parks and it's also possible to take the free ferry from Stenpiren to Lindholmen and walk the short distance. Frihamnen was the second to last stop for competitors in the Volvo Ocean Race in 2018 and was flocked with spectators eager to see teams maneuver sailboats into port.

30. HARBOR & GÖTA RIVER LOUNGING

When arriving at Järntorget, if you gravitate toward the harbor and are hankering for a place to sit and fixate on the waterway's industrial landscape, you will find an outdoor space designed by architects from the collective This Side Up. In cooperation with city's parking bureau, the group re-shaped part of the waterfront of Gothenburg at Masthuggskajen by introducing a space where pop-up parks, enhanced landscaping, social sitting and diverse activities could take place. It's located to the right on the Stena Line cruise terminal if looking at the water. The exciting, colorful installation is a way for locals to organize and share ideas while lounging in the wooden modules.

Just a short walk away going toward Stenpiren transport hub, you can lounge in a different setting on reclining chairs and ponder your next site to visit. The unsuspecting metal umbrellas will undoubtedly withstand the gusts should the wind pick up, but if it's sunny, you'll see many people here basking in the sun.

>TOURIST

31. FESKEKÔRKA

Feskekôrka, or Fish Church, is an iconic mainstay of Gothenburg and was anointed the name by its uncanny resemblance to a Neo-gothic church. The landmark has no religious affiliation due to the fact that it's a fish market and sells some of the freshest catch in Gothenburg. The building dates back to 1874 and was designed by the city architect Victor von Gegerfelt. Worth a stroll within its walls, the indoor fish market is an institution which houses one of the city's oldest trades: fishing.

On the top floor of Feskekôrka is a unique seafood restaurant called Restaurang Gabriel, that overlooks the market hall and serves some of the best ocean catches of the day. The lunch menu varies daily depending on the season and availability. The restaurant isn't open for dinner, so consider shucking some oysters or indulging in the seafood buffet for an afternoon meal. Right next to the market and adjoining the canal is a lounge area with oversized reclining chairs to sit and relax on if the time is right.

32. LAKE VISITS

Delsjön is a tranquil reserve with a lake free of any motorized vessels and a network of trails running through the forest. You can jump on the 10 tram and get off at Töpelsgatan, arriving two kilometers from the lake, or about a 20 to 25-minute trek. You'll find crisp water to dip into, a volleyball net, picnic and barbequing areas, and kayaking opportunities. In the winter, the cascading hill that ends at the water's edge becomes a sledding zone and locals also flock to the area for some steadfast cross-country skiing. It's possible to take a fika break at one of the cafes located in the park.

Kåsjön is a smaller lake, but also a popular swimming hole and has diving boards that thrill seekers can scale to plunge into the fresh waters. There are a few types of terrain found around the lake such as long sandy beaches, rocky hills, and grassy knolls. This body of water is permissible for boats, sailing, windsurfing and kitesurfing. The trails in this wilderness are narrow and swooping, encased by dramatic gorges and barren hills, surrounded by a deciduous forest.

\>TOURIST

33. SHOPPING

Gothenburg is a very fashion-conscious city and you'll find a wide assortment of styles when walking down the street. Nordstan and Arkaden Galleria shopping malls, and surrounding areas have a blend of native brands and international influences heavily concentrated around Kungsportplatsen (where the statue of King Charles IX riding a horse is) and Brunnsparken nearby the moat. As Swedes love their regional Scandinavian design aesthetic, there are many stores which sell interior design goods, along with some vending patriotic souvenirs decorated with the Swedish flag, moose, their royal family, and other quintessential motifs that define the country.

If your budget is tight or you prefer clothes with a mysterious backstory, then you'll be relieved to know that Gothenburg is rich in secondhand shops. One the largest is Myrorna, a multi-story abyss of literally thousands of articles of clothing, décor, books and more. A similar but smaller-scale shop is not far from Myrorna, called Emmaus Björkå, and has an impressive number of shoes to choose from, along with all genres of attire and trinkets.

Bebop in Haga is a vintage shop specialized in Scandinavian design, primarily from 1920 to 1970.

They have furniture and lamps, but also, jewelry, textiles, ceramics and more. Even if you don't plan to transport a nearly hundred-year-old lamp back home, this shop is similar to a gallery of famous Scandinavian design.

34. MAJORNA DISTRICT

Majorna has positioned itself as the up-and-coming neighborhood in Gothenburg, leading grassroots initiatives for urban farming and cultural consciousness, and luring many to take up residence in the lively district. From Järntorget, you can hop onto tram 3 which will take you through the main avenue up to Mariaplatsen, where faddish restaurants such as Enoteca Maglia and cafés such as the green oasis of Materia can be discovered. Views of the Göta Älv river and the Röda Sten Art Centre are located in Majorna as well.

The district has several vintage and secondhand shops, staying true to its dubbed hipster character. Fabriken has a selection of goods dating back to the 1900s and also vends locally manufactured goods. Bengans Records store has vintage goods and rare LP-records for sale, while also

\>TOURIST

housing a café to enjoy the old-fashioned setting. Musikens Hus is a music hall, restaurant and bar with vegetarian food, solid music and local beer. The venue also coordinates courses in dance and music that can be attended for a fee. Music performances are generally planned a few days a week and usually have free admission.

As for the structural integrity of the neighborhood, many typical "county governor" houses are lining the streets, designed with the ground floor made of stone, and a second and third upper floors constructed in wood, due to fire regulations. Gathenhielmska Huset is a wooden two-story house with a steep hipped roof, built in a Late Baroque style and completed in 1747. The building is protected and preserved, serving as the only one in Gothenburg from that time. It might not seem like much to some, but it's an esteemed structure.

35. CRAFT BEER & MICROBREWERIES

In the union of industrial and hipster spirits of Gothenburg, it's logical that the city has become a major player in Sweden as the hub of microbreweries. Tellingly, since the city was founded in 1621, there have been breweries concocting their poisons locally. In 2017, Gothenburg India Pale Ales made Ratebeers' list of the world's 50 best new beers, with two of the beers created by Stigberget one from O/O Brewing. Considering the tens of thousands of beers entered for the prize, it demonstrates the quality of brews coming from the city.

Establishments in Gothenburg typically keep a healthy selection of bottled beers and also on tap, but Tullen (there are several locations in the city) maintains a beer collection that entirely originats from Sweden. Dugges and Poppels are just two brands that offer an assortment of beers ranging from lagers and ales to porter. Having some drinks at home can be facilitated by a trip to Systembolaget (the liquor store chain) which has boatloads of beer ready to be bottom up. Note that the opening hours at Systembolaget are limited, so it's wise to plan ahead for the evening, otherwise you'll be buying beer from the grocery stores which by law can only be of a lower alcohol percentage.

Omnipollo is a phantom brewery in the midst of Linnéstan, unleashing nuanced recipes which has earned them a number six ranking on Ratebeer's list of the world's best beer producers in 2017. The popcorn flavored beer could be one of the most obscure beers available on location, but there are descriptions for their beers on tap displayed clearly so you can try a variety of tastes. The spot is small and a good place to pop in for a drink or two before venturing to the next stop.

36. IT'S RAINING, COULD BE POURING

Take a trip to IKEA to browse the Scandinavian designs that supply an exorbitant number of Swedes close to their entire interior décor. While you're there, you can dine in the eateries and order some of the notorious foods associated with IKEA: meatballs and hotdogs.

Should you want a form of entertainment in the way of games, Biljardpalatset is the best spot to go for a round of pool or shuffleboard. The atmosphere is warm and ample, with two floors of 18 shuffleboard games and 30 billiard tables, and a restaurant and bar focused on Swedish flavors although accompanied by influences from North America and France.

Not in the mood for competition and wanting to relax in a cushioned chair while images dance on a screen? There are a few movie theaters to choose from in the city, but the largest one is SF Filmstaden Bergakungen and has 14 cinemas that show a mix of English and Swedish language films. There's a VIP cinema with an adjacent lounge and a bar with an intimate ambiance. The Göta bio (movie theater) located at Götaplatsen is quaint and features an employee that gives a brief synopsis of the movie in Swedish beforehand; even though you might not understand, it still brings a charming element to the experience.

37. NORTHERN ARCHIPELAGO

The northern archipelago is reachable by car and you can also access the islands by a car ferry from Lilla Varholmen at Hisingen. You can use one of the free yellow road ferries that depart from Lilla

>TOURIST

Varholmen (Hjuvik) on the western tip of Torslanda and they will take you to either Hönö or Bjorkö.

Öckerö and Hönö Klåva are easy islands to get to and scenic environments that can be explored, coupled with quaint residential neighborhoods that you can check out. There is a ferry from Stenpiren to Hönö Klåva in the summer which is a nice island with restaurants, shopping, coffee, and swimming. Gothenburg's most westerly point is the island of Vinga and has a legendary lighthouse and stunning nature, and can be reached by boats launching from Hönö.

38. ESPERANTOPLATSEN

English is widely spoken throughout Gothenburg, as Swedes begin to learn early on and sometimes work or study using the language, but there is also a variety of mother tongues spoken in the city. If you're interested in picking up another language or want to practice a previously acquired one, the Språkcaféet (language café) is a hub to meet likeminded language learners in the evenings during the week. It's location is central at Esperanto plaza, which can be found easily using the blue tower from the Gothenburg

Energy building across the street as a landmark. The café's website outlines which days focus on certain languages and the only stipulation to participate is spending at least 45 kronor.

If you aren't up for a laborious conversation in a foreign language but still end up passing by, you'll be able to see part of the only remaining fortifications built by Swedish and Dutch engineers to protect the city. The last remnants of the Carolus Rex bastion are lofty stone walls dating back to the 17th century and are incorporated into the natural landscape, constructed inside the moat that surrounds part of the city. Just a short walk away, down the street, Rosenlundsgatan, you'll see a frequented lunch spot called Barabicu which dubs itself as a Pan American eatery with a relaxed atmosphere. If the weather is right, dining in the heat of the sun could be surprisingly comfortable and welcomed.

>TOURIST

39. MARITIME MUSEUM & VOLVO MUSEUM

These two exhibitions offer extremely opposite experiences, but they both represent determining identities for the city of Gothenburg. The Maritime Museum can be reached easily as it is located just behind the Opera House. The town's celebrated vessels are moored to the dock and for a nominal fee, visitors can navigate the upper and lower decks of nearly 20 vessels and imagine what life could be like on the high seas. The collection is impressive even from shore if you can't devote the cash to explore inside. The museum is generally not open from November to March.

The Volvo Museum epitomizes one of Gothenburg's most well-known brands and takes you on an evolution of the car most commonly driven in the city. The facility has 8,000 square meters of cars, buses, machines, engines and unique concepts for visitors to marvel at, along with exhibitions on the Volvo Ocean Race and Volvo Golf Experience. The museum is a historical time capsule of Volvo manufacturing since the start in 1927, and located a short journey on the island of Hisingen. Take the closest transport, most likely with a transfer or two, to

Arendals Skans stop and then it will be a short walk to the museum.

40. FALL FESTIVITIES

Autumn is a beautiful time in Gothenburg as the landscape takes on dramatic color transformations from vibrant greens to fall hues. Haga Farmer's Market brings together local growers selling their bounty at the heart of Haga Nygata street. There are a number of products locally made and sold at the market, which is held every Saturday from 10:00 – 2:00 p.m. starting at the beginning of August and running until the end of October. People have also set up stalls to sell odds and ends, clothing, and maybe even something they've had in their attic for decades.

Ringön's street fair takes place at Järnmalmsgatan along the sea and is a flea market with art, music and food. The spread of cuisine is international and made authentically by people from all across the globe. This event has a very relaxed, open scene, with people dancing in the street and living their best lives. The area is a mix of businesses and industrial warehouse, some of which have become art galleries. The district has been expanding organically in order to attract more residents while also upholding the local character of the zone. Once night falls, there's usually an outdoor screening with works from the Göteborg Film Festival.

Popular activities in the fall include Halloween at Liseberg where the tiny town is transformed into a spooky fright fest for both children and adults. For the past 25 years in October, Gothenburg has hosted a festival called Kulturnatta (Culture Night) scattered around the city and incorporates a broad mix of activities, art, music, theatre and everything in between. The event is free of charge and naturally there are events that fit non-Swedish speaking guests. The city of Gothenburg puts forth a noble effort in bringing people together through events like this and encourages all to join in. Search Kulturnatta to see the date and browse a program of the events.

41. CITY JUBILEES

Gothenburg event planning must be a juggling act in order to fit in the amount of festivals and events arranged in the city. During January and February, the city strategically coordinates the Göteborg Film Festival, one of the leading film festivals in the Nordic countries. The cinematic list is published online and features film in different languages from all over the world and with subtitles. This is a gratifying way to stay indoors during the dead of winter.

During summer, festivals engulf the city with amazing displays of culture, food, workshops, parades, and more. EuroPride is an annual recurring event and one of the designated Pride Festival locations in Europe able to use the title. Rapture and inclusivity are celebrated in the week-long joyous occasion with conferences, conversations, information sessions, workshops and concludes with a closing ceremony at Götaplatsen following the massive EuroPride Parade.

In 2018, Gothenburg Culture Festival took place the same week as EuroPride, and set up 1,200 free activities open for everyone to experience, ranging from opera, art, music, theatre, handicrafts, literature

> TOURIST

and more. There are also food trucks offering international cuisines cooked authentically by local establishments or people in grassroots initiatives looking to bring communities together by food.

42. ARCHITECTURE

Historical buildings in Gothenburg sometimes blend in with surrounding facades since the city is covered in beautiful, ornate long-standing edifices. If you want to find some of the oldest, most preserved structures, it's wise to investigate what they look like online to give you better reference, but the downtown area is covered in old structures if you enjoy just meandering around.

Two of Gothenburg's oldest streets are Norra Hamngatan and Södra Hamngatan, so taking a walk along these avenues could be an independent historical tour through the city on its own. Residenset or The Residency is located at Södra Hamngatan 1 (close the city museum and moat) and is the oldest residential building in Gothenburg, completed in 1651. The Dutch Renaissance style house kept both royals and governors over the years.

43. NEW YEAR'S EVE

New Year's Eve is an energetic time where Swedes embrace the cold weather in their best garbs and make a memorable evening with friends or family. Some locals will choose to opt for a house party and cram into an apartment or home, or venture out to a member of the crew's family's summer house, but many will take to the streets, waiting in line to get into their preferred club or meet up at their usual stomping grounds if they're open.

The local newspaper puts on an extravagant fireworks show earlier in the evening (around 5 p.m. since it's dark by then) over the harbor and many people gather at Stenpiren Transit Hub or the Opera House to watch from the decks. This isn't a party, but merely a festivity where friends and family watch some explosives from a safe distance. It's common to see the fireworks and then go back home to get ready before heading out if you don't have dinner plans.

Restaurants will be filled with folks who have either made reservations long in advance or have stumbled across the right place at the right time. That being said, if you plan to have a nice dinner, it's best to call (English is always an option) and reserve a table at a place instead of trying to find one that night.

> TOURIST

If the clubs on Avenyn aren't your scene, Jazzhuset, Pustervik or Henriksberg could be possible alternatives for music and dancing.

44. MARSTRAND

Marstrand is the west coast sailing metropolis of Sweden and hosts the Marstrand Regatta, Match Cup Sweden and other major sailing championships. When these events aren't going on, the picturesque island is a prime location for a stroll through nature and history. At the pinnacle of the island is Carlstens Fästning, a fortress partly completed by convicts sentenced to hard labor in the 1660s after the Swedish takeover of Bohuslän. You can pay admission to explore the grounds of the fortress, its secret tunnel and prison cells, and the view from the top provides sweeping panoramas of the archipelago. While visiting the fortress, it's crucial to learn about the story of Lasse Maja, a cross-dressing thief, who is notorious in the region for his tricks.

Not feeling like a history lesson? The island can be circumnavigated in a short time and will take you through trails and the old town. It's possible to go on a fishing or seal excursions, as well as swim off shore if the weather is agreeable. There are also some restaurants and bars on the island, along with the Strandverket Art Museum housed in an old fort. Should you have extra time and resources, the Marstrand Havshotell has a relaxing spa with hot and cold dips and saunas. You can get to Marstrand by bus or by a boat tour leaving from Lilla Bommen.

45. LONG-DISTANCE TRANSPORT

Taking private transportation like taxis and Ubers can get expensive in Gothenburg, and although you wouldn't typically take them long distance, it's nice to know of more economic options when planning your travels. There are comfortable and inexpensive buses that carry passengers to and from Landvetter airport, which is about 20 minutes from the main bus and tram hubs. Depending on if you're staying closer to Korsvägen or Kungsportplaten, you can find the airport shuttle and buy your ticket at a kiosk ahead of time. You'll save a bit of cash if you buy the roundtrip ticket and buses leave about every 15 minutes from both the airport and the stations. Find

>TOURIST

out which stop is closest to where you're staying and then you will be able to walk or find transport easily.

Backpackers might like to enjoy traveling by ferry to various countries in Europe from one of the Stena Line ships docked in port close to Järntorget. There are varying accommodations and prices depending on the route, so it's best to check out prices on the Stena Line website which is also in English. Gothenburg Central Station is your jumping off point for long-distance trains and buses if you'd like to visit Stockholm, Oslo or Copenhagen, for example, which are within a few hours of Gothenburg.

46. VASASTAN DISTRICT

This area is mostly composed of beautiful stone houses dating back to between 1870 to 1920, with neo-renaissance and baroque styles that influenced the architecture. Vasastan depicts one of Gothenburg's most characteristic neighborhoods which was formally one of the first middle-class residential areas outside the moat. The area has a lively, youthful feel to it considering the proximity of one of the Gothenburg University campuses and it's string of establishments and art galleries, along with Röhsska Museum.

Along the street, Götabergsgatan, you'll pass a number of galleries and in the midst of strolling along you'll see a number of places to grab a beer. Bord 27 is lauded for being a family-owned restaurant conscious about serving food at affordable prices. The beloved neighborhood restaurant has a laid-back energy and adapts their servings to accommodate all kinds of eaters with dishes big and small. Happy M Kitchen concerns itself with serving mostly organic ingredients in its meals and beverages, and offers cooking courses to demonstrate ways to prepare tasty, clean food.

>TOURIST

47. NATURE OUTSIDE THE CITY

You can take a short ride out of the city center and reach the countryside and slower-paced place replete of untouched nature and beauty. If you enjoy trekking on trails or just taking a jog in the serene backcountry, there are a number of locations that can be reached by public transportation such as Billdals Park and Lärjeån Valley.

Southwest of the city center is where Billdals park is located and is bordered by mountains and forests. It would be nice to bring a picnic and enjoy the wilderness in this area, as there are waterways and trails to explore shaded by deciduous trees. Lärjeån is a valley rife of abundant natural value with lush forests and rich vegetation and wildlife. and is. There are wooded hills and deciduous forests are partially protected and swimming in the river there are both trout and salmon. There is a 7.5 km-long nature trail, several routes, and horse paths.

Swedes take great pride in their heritage of picking berries and mushrooms, and they're allowed to enjoy the Earth's bounty anywhere they please in the country. So, while out, if you identify (edible) berries or mushrooms, take advantage of the fresh access to lingonberries, raspberries or other harvests.

48. ACCOMMODATION

Booking you trip for the months of August or September far in advance might be beneficial. During these months you'll find many people scattered about Gothenburg looking for places to stay since it's the start of the semester for the two universities in town. To the dismay of many, there is a severe housing shortage in the city which oftentimes leaves students scrambling for accommodation and staying in Airbnbs for the interim until they can find proper housing. That being said, if you're used to renting Airbnbs, the options might be limited at this time, so be mindful when planning ahead and looking for a place to stay. Otherwise, there are countless hotels, hostels and other accommodation scattered all over the city center.

49. SPORTING EVENTS

If you happen to land in Gothenburg during a televised sporting event, there are a few places that set the atmosphere for competition. O'Leary's is a popular American-style sports bar with flat screens at every angle. If the sport is one that Swedes are interested in, such as football (soccer) or hockey, then count on reserving a table in advance, otherwise you will be relegated to whatever standing room remains. If the crowds aren't conducive to following the game at O'Leary's, you can take a seat at John Scott's which has a wide selection of beers and pub food and is usually less busy.

The city's professional football (soccer) teams are IFK Göteborg, GAIS and BK Häcken, and play at the Gamla Ullevi and Bravida Arena stadiums between April and November. The tickets aren't too pricey and the proximity to the pitch allows spectators to view an exciting match up close. If you're more intrigued by people watching than the players, it's entertaining to look at and listen to the football fanatics beat their drums and chant their tunes. Frölunda Hockey Club, also dubbed the Frölunda Indians, is a professional Swedish ice hockey club grounded in Gothenburg. They compete in the highest national league and typically square-off in the Scandinavium arena starting from the season opener in September until March.

In July, international youth soccer squads are teeming the city streets when they're not playing in matches. Heden is the main location for the annual Gothia World Youth Cup and Partille Cup, so don't be alarmed if you see joyful droves of youngsters in the public transport. Heden sports complex is massive and also has ice skating in the winter, a basketball court, playground, and mini-golf open to the public.

>TOURIST

50. MAGASINSGATAN AREA

Magasinsgatan is a trendy district with some of the finest cafés, and a vibe conducive to a blend of Swedish fashion brands, secondhand shops, food trucks and expensive boutiques. Da Matteo is regarded as having some of the best coffee in town and directly next to the café is the interior design paradise, Artilleriet, which bodes remarkable works of art, but not without a lofty price tag. It's still enjoyable to peruse the store if you fancy that.

Food trucks often park in the square to sell their cuisines, one being Strömmingsluckan, which vends Swedish classics such as herring, mashed potatoes and lingonberries. If you've already eaten and taken a fika, the area has some beautiful murals to admire instead. If you do end up making a purchase, though, you can practice some polite Swedish and say "tack" or "tack så mycket" when thanking merchants, and you can also bid them farewell, telling them to take care, saying "ha det bra!". You might be excited to hear a deep Gothenburg dialect in return wishing you the equivalent, with a "ha det gôtt!". Then it's up to you whether you'd like to employ the local dialect or stick to the mainstream, but regardless, those few words will get you a long way in Sweden.

>TOURIST

TOP REASONS TO BOOK THIS TRIP

Culture: The city has a vibrant culture, with fresh seafood and engagement.

Nature: The urban green spaces and archipelago are captivating and accessible.

Activities: There are constantly events and shows in Gothenburg.

BONUS BOOK

50 THINGS TO KNOW ABOUT PACKING LIGHT FOR TRAVEL

PACK THE RIGHT WAY EVERY TIME

AUTHOR: MANIDIPA BHATTACHARYYA

First Published in 2015 by Dr. Lisa Rusczyk. Copyright 2015. All Rights Reserved. No part of this publication may be reproduced, including scanning and photocopying, or distributed in any form or by any means, electronic or mechanical, or stored in a database or retrieval system without prior written permission from the publisher.

Disclaimer: The publisher has put forth an effort in preparing and arranging this book. The information provided herein by the author is provided "as is". Use this information at your own risk. The publisher is not a licensed doctor. Consult your doctor before engaging in any medical activities. The publisher and author disclaim any liabilities for any loss of profit or commercial or personal damages resulting from the information contained in this book.

Edited by Melanie Howthorne

ABOUT THE AUTHOR

Manidipa Bhattacharyya is a creative writer and editor, with an education in English literature and Linguistics. After working in the IT industry for seven long years she decided to call it quits and follow her heart instead. Manidipa has been ghost writing, editing, proof reading and doing secondary research services for many story tellers and article writers for about three years. She stays in Kolkata, India with her husband and a busy two year old. In her own time Manidipa enjoys travelling, photography and writing flash fiction.

Manidipa believes in travelling light and never carries anything that she couldn't haul herself on a trip. However, travelling with her child changed the scenario. She seemed to carry the entire world with her for the baby on the first two trips. But good sense prevailed and she is again working her way to becoming a light traveler, this time with a kid.

INTRODUCTION

*He who would travel happily
must travel light.*

-Antoine de Saint-Exupéry

Travel takes you to different places from seas and mountains to deserts and much more. In your travels you get to interact with different people and their cultures. You will, however, enjoy the sights and interact positively with these new people even more, if you are travelling light.

When you travel light your mind can be free from worry about your belongings. You do not have to spend precious vacation time waiting for your luggage to arrive after a long flight. There is be no chance of your bags going missing and the best part is that you need not pay a fee for checked baggage.

People who have mastered this art of packing light will root for you to take only one carry-on, wherever you go. However, many people can find it really hard to pack light. More so if you are travelling with children. Differentiating between "must have" and "just in case" items is the starting point. There will be ample shopping avenues at your destination which are just waiting to be explored.

This book will show you 'packing' in a new 'light' – pun intended – and help you to embrace light packing practices for all of your future travels.

Off to packing!

DEDICATION

I dedicate this book to all the travel buffs that I know, who have given me great insights into the contents of their backpacks.

THE RIGHT TRAVEL GEAR

1. CHOOSE YOUR TRAVEL GEAR CAREFULLY

While selecting your travel gear, pick items that are light weight, durable and most importantly, easy to carry. There are cases with wheels so you can drag them along – these are usually on the heavy side because of the trolley. Alternatively a backpack that you can carry comfortably on your back, or even a duffel bag that you can carry easily by hand or sling across your body are also great options. Whatever you choose, one thing to keep in mind is that the luggage itself should not weigh a ton, this will give you the flexibility to bring along one extra pair of shoes if you so desire.

2. CARRY THE MINIMUM NUMBER OF BAGS

Selecting light weight luggage is not everything. You need to restrict the number of bags you carry as well. One carry-on size bag is ideal for light travel. Most carriers allow one cabin baggage plus one purse, handbag or camera bag as long as it slides under the seat in front. So technically, you can carry two items of luggage without checking them in.

3. PACK ONE EXTRA BAG

Always pack one extra empty bag along with your essential items. This could be a very light weight duffel bag or even a sturdy tote bag which takes up minimal space. In the event that you end up buying a lot of souvenirs, you already have a handy bag to stuff all that into and do not have to spend time hunting for an appropriate bag.

> *I'm very strict with my packing and have everything in its right place. I never change a rule. I hardly use anything in the hotel room. I wheel my own wardrobe in and that's it.*
>
> Charlie Watts

CLOTHES & ACCESSORIES

4. PLAN AHEAD

Figure out in advance what you plan to do on your trip. That will help you to pick that one dress you need for the occasion. If you are going to attend a wedding then you have to carry formal wear. If not, you can ditch the gown for something lighter that will be comfortable during long walks or on the beach.

5. WEAR THAT JACKET

Remember that wearing items will not add extra luggage for your air travel. So wear that bulky jacket that you plan to carry for your trip. This saves space and can also help keep you warm during the chilly flight.

6. MIX AND MATCH

Carry clothes that can be interchangeably used to reinvent your look. Find one top that goes well with a couple of pairs of pants or skirts. Use tops, shirts and jackets wisely along with other accessories like a scarf or a stole to create a new look.

7. CHOOSE YOUR FABRIC WISELY

Stuffing clothes in cramped bags definitely takes its toll which results in wrinkles. It is best to carry wrinkle free, synthetic clothes or merino tops. This will eliminate the need for that small iron you usually bring along.

8. DITCH CLOTHES PACK UNDERWEAR

Pack more underwear and socks. These are the things that will give you a fresh feel even if you do not get a chance to wear fresh clothes. Moreover these are easy to wash and can be dried inside the hotel room itself.

9. CHOOSE DARK OVER LIGHT

While picking your clothes choose dark coloured ones. They are easy to colour coordinate and can last longer before needing a wash. Accidental food spills and dirt from the road are less visible on darker clothes.

10. WEAR YOUR JEANS

Take only one pair of Jeans with you, which you should wear on the flight. Remember to pick a pair that can be worn for sightseeing trips and is equally eloquent for dinner. You can add variety by adding light weight cargoes and chinos.

11. CARRY SMART ACCESSORIES

The right accessory can give you a fresh look even with the same old dress. An intelligent neck-piece, a couple of bright scarves, stoles or a sarong can be used in a number of ways to add variety to your clothing. These light weight beauties can double up as a nursing cover, a light blanket, beach wear, a modesty cover for visiting places of worship, and also makes for an enthralling game of peek-a-boo.

12. LEARN TO FOLD YOUR GARMENTS

Seasoned travellers all swear by rolling their clothes for compact and wrinkle free packing. Bundle packing, where you roll the clothes around a central object as if tying it up, is also a popular method of compact and wrinkle free packing. Stacking folded clothes one on top of another is a big no-no as it makes creases extreme and they are difficult to get rid of without ironing.

13. WASH YOUR DIRTY LAUNDRY

One of the ways to avoid carrying loads of clothes is to wash the clothes you carry. At some places you might get to use the laundry services or a Laundromat but if you are in a pinch, best solution is to wash them yourself. If that is the plan then carrying quick drying clothes is highly recommended, which most often also happen to be the wrinkle free variety.

14. LEAVE THOSE TOWELS BEHIND

Regular towels take up a lot of space, are heavy and take ages to dry out. If you are staying at hotels they will provide you with towels anyway. If you are travelling to a remote place, where the availability of towels look doubtful, carry a light weight travel towel of viscose material to do the job.

15. USE A COMPRESSION BAG

Compression bags are getting lots of recommendation now days from regular travellers. These are useful for saving space in your luggage when you have to pack bulky dresses. While packing for the return trip, get help from the hotel staff to arrange a vacuum cleaner.

FOOTWEAR

16. PUT ON YOUR HIKING BOOTS

If you have plans to go hiking or trekking during your trip, you will need those bulky hiking boots. The best way to carry them is to wear them on flight to save space and luggage weight. You can remove the boots once inside and be comfortable in your socks.

17. PICKING THE RIGHT SHOES

Shoes are often the bulkiest items, along with being the dainty if you are a female. They need care and take up a lot of space in your luggage. It is advisable therefore to pick shoes very carefully. If you plan to do a lot of walking and site seeing, then wearing a pair of comfortable walking shoes are a must. For more formal occasions you can carry durable, light weight flats which will not take up much space.

18. STUFF SHOES

If you happen to pack a pair of shoes, ensure you utilize their hollow insides. Tuck small items like rolled up socks or belts to save space. They will also be easy to find.

>TOURIST

TOILETRIES

19. STASHING TOILETRIES

Carry only absolute necessities. Airline rules dictate that for one carry-on bag, liquids and gels must be in 3.4 ounce (100ml) bottles or less, and must be packed in a one quart zip-lock bag. If you are planning to stay in a hotel, the basic things will be provided for you. It's best is to buy the rest from the local market at your destination.

20. TAKE ALONG TAMPONS

Tampons are a hard to find item in a lot of countries. Figure out how many you need and pack accordingly. For longer stays you can buy them online and have them delivered to where you are staying.

21. GET PAMPERED BEFORE YOU TRAVEL

Some avid travellers suggest getting a pedicure and manicure just the day before travelling. This not only gives you a well kept look, you also save the trouble of packing nail polish. Remember, every little bit of weight reduced adds up.

ELECTRONICS

22. LUGGING ALONG ELECTRONICS

Electronics have a large role to play in our lives today. Most of us cannot imagine our lives away from our phones, laptops or tablets. However while travelling, one must consider the amount of weight these electronics add to our luggage. Thankfully smart phones come along with all the essentials tools like a camera, email access, picture editing tools and more. They are smart to the point of eliminating the need to carry multiple gadgets. Choose a smart phone that suits all your requirements and travel with the world in your palms or pocket.

23. REDUCE THE NUMBER OF CHARGERS

If you do travel with multiple electronic devices, you will have to bear the additional burden of carrying all their chargers too. Check if a single charger can be used for multiple devices. You might also consider investing in a pocket charger. These small devices support multiple devices while keeping you charged on the go.

> TOURIST

24. TRAVEL FRIENDLY APPS

Along with smart phones come numerous apps, which are immensely helpful in our travels. You name it and you have an app for it at hand – take pictures, sharing with friends and family, torch to light dark roads, maps, checking flight/train times, find hotels and many other things. Use these smart alternatives to traditional items like books to eliminate weight and save space.

> *I get ideas about what's essential when packing my suitcase.*

-Diane von Furstenberg

TRAVELLING WITH KIDS

25. BRING ALONG THE STROLLER

Kids might enjoy walking for a while but they soon tire out and a stroller is the just the right thing for them to rest in while you continue your tour. Strollers also double duty as a luggage carrier and shopping bag holder. Remember to pick a light weight, easy to handle brand of stroller. Better yet, find out in advance if you can rent a stroller at your destination.

26. BRING ONLY ENOUGH DIAPERS FOR YOUR TRIP

Diapers take up a lot of space and add to the weight of your luggage. Therefore it is advisable to carry just enough diapers to last through the trip and a few for afterwards, till you buy fresh stock at your destination. Unless of course you are travelling to a really remote area, in which case you have no choice but to carry the load. Otherwise diapers are something you will find pretty easily.

27. TAKE ONLY A COUPLE OF TOYS

Children are easily attracted by new things in their environment. While travelling they will find numerous 'new' objects to scrutinize and play with. Packing just one favorite toy is enough, or if there is no favorite toy leave out all of them in favor of stories or imaginary games.

28. CARRY KID FRIENDLY SNACKS

Create a small snack counter in your bag to store away quick bites for those sudden hunger pangs. Depending on the child's age this could include chocolates, raisins, dry fruits, granola bars or biscuits. Also keep a bottle of water handy for your little one.

>TOURIST

These things do not add much weight and can be adjusted in a handbag or knapsack.

29. GAMES TO CARRY

Create some travel specific, imaginary games if you have slightly grown up children, like spot the attractions. Keep a coloring book and colors handy for in-flight or hotel time. Apps on your smart phone can keep the children engaged with cartoons and story books. Older children are often entertained by games available on phones or tablets. This cuts the weight of luggage down while keeping the kids entertained.

30. LET THE KIDS CARRY THEIR LOAD

A good thing is to start early sharing of responsibilities. Let your child pick a bag of his or her choice and pack it themselves. Keep tabs on what they are stuffing in their bags by asking if they will be using that item on the trip. It could start out being just an entertainment bag initially but with growing years they will learn to sort the useful from the superfluous. Children as little as four can maneuver a small trolley suitcase like a pro- their experience in pull along toys credit. If you are worried that you may be pulling it for them, you may want to start with a backpack.

31. DECIDE ON LOCATION FOR CHILDREN TO SLEEP

While on a trip you might not always get a crib at your destination, and carrying one will make life all the more difficult. Instead call ahead to see if there are any cribs or roll out beds for children. You may even put blankets on the floor. Weave them a story about camping and they will gladly sleep without any trouble.

32. GET BABY PRODUCTS DELIVERED AT YOUR DESTINATION

If you are absolutely paranoid about not getting your favourite variety of diaper or brand of baby food, check out online stores like amazon.com for services in your destination city. You can buy things online ahead of your travel and get them delivered to your hotel upon arrival.

33. FEEDING NEEDS OF YOUR INFANTS

If you are travelling with a breastfed infant, you save the trouble of carrying bottles and bottle sanitization kits. For special food, or medications, you may need to call ahead to make sure you have a refrigerator where you are staying.

34. FEEDING NEEDS OF YOUR TODDLER

With the progression from infancy to toddler, their dietary requirements too evolve. You will have to pack some snacks for travelling time. Fresh fruits and vegetables can be purchased at your destination. Most of the cities you travel to in whichever part of the world, will have baby food products and formulas, available at the local drug-store or the supermarket.

35. PICKING CLOTHES FOR YOUR BABY

Contrary to popular belief, babies can do without many changes of clothes. At the most pack 2 outfits per day. Pack mix and match type clothes for your little one as well. Pick things which are comfortable to wear and quick to dry.

36. SELECTING SHOES FOR YOUR BABY

Like outfits, kids can make do with two pairs of comfortable shoes. If you can get some water resistant shoes it will be best. To expedite drying wet shoes, you can stuff newspaper in them then wrap them with newspaper and leave them to dry overnight.

37. KEEP ONE CHANGE OF CLOTHES HANDY

Travelling with kids can be tricky. Keep a change of clothes for the kids and mum handy in your purse or tote bag. This takes a bit of space in your hand luggage but comes extremely handy in case there are any accidents or spills.

38. LEAVE BEHIND BABY ACCESSORIES

Baby accessories like their bed, bath tub, car seat, crib etc. should be left at home. Many hotels provide a crib on request, while car seats can be borrowed from friends or rented. Babies can be given a bath in the hotel sink or even in the adult bath tub with a little bit of water. If you bring a few bath toys, they can be used in the bath, pool, and out of water. They can also be sanitized easily in the sink.

39. CARRY A SMALL LOAD OF PLASTIC BAGS

With children around there are chances of a number of soiled clothes and diapers. These plastic bags help to sort the dirt from the clean inside your big bag.

>TOURIST

These are very light weight and come in handy to other carry stuff as well at times.

PACK WITH A PURPOSE

40. PACKING FOR BUSINESS TRIPS

One neutral-colored suit should suffice. It can be paired with different shirts, ties and accessories for different occasions. One pair of black suit pants could be worn with a matching jacket for the office or with a snazzy top for dinner.

41. PACKING FOR A CRUISE

Most cruises have formal dinners, and that formal dress usually takes up a lot of space. However you might find a tuxedo to rent. For women, a short black dress with multiple accessory options will do the trick.

42. PACKING FOR A LONG TRIP OVER DIFFERENT CLIMATES

The secret packing mantra for travel over multiple climates is layering. Layering traps air around your body creating insulation against the cold. The same light t-shirt that is comfortable in a warmer climate can be the innermost layer in a colder climate.

REDUCE SOME MORE WEIGHT

43. LEAVE PRECIOUS THINGS AT HOME

Things that you would hate to lose or get damaged leave them at home. Precious jewelry, expensive gadgets or dresses, could be anything. You will not require these on your trip. Leave them at home and spare the load on your mind.

44. SEND SOUVENIRS BY MAIL

If you have spent all your money on purchasing souvenirs, carrying them back in the same bag that you brought along would be difficult. Either pack everything in another bag and check it in the airport or get everything shipped to your home. Use an international carrier for a secure transit, but this could be more expensive than the checking fees at the airport.

45. AVOID CARRYING BOOKS

Books equal to weight. There are many reading apps which you can download on your smart phone or tab.

Plus there are gadgets like Kindle and Nook that are thinner and lighter alternatives to your regular book.

CHECK, GET, SET, CHECK AGAIN

46. STRATEGIZE BEFORE PACKING

Create a travel list and prepare all that you think you need to carry along. Keep everything on your bed or floor before packing and then think through once again – do I really need that? Any item that meets this question can be avoided. Remove whatever you don't really need and pack the rest.

47. TEST YOUR LUGGAGE

Once you have fully packed for the trip take a test trip with your luggage. Take your bags and go to town for window shopping for an hour. If you enjoy your hour long trip it is good to go, if not, go home and reduce the load some more. Repeat this test till you hit the right weight.

48. ADD A ROLL OF DUCT TAPE

You might wonder why, when this book has been talking about reducing stuff, we're suddenly asking you to pack something totally unusual. This is because when you have limited supplies, duct tape is immensely helpful for small repairs – a broken bag, leaking zip-lock bag, broken sunglasses, you name it and duct tape can fix it, temporarily.

49. LIST OF ESSENTIAL ITEMS

Even though the emphasis is on packing light, there are things which have to be carried for any trip. Here is our list of essentials:

- Passport/Visa or any other ID

- Any other paper work that might be required on a trip like permits, hotel reservation confirmations etc.

- Medicines – all your prescription medicines and emergency kit, especially if you are travelling with children

- Medical or vaccination records

- Money in foreign currency if travelling to a different country

- Tickets- Email or Message them to your phone

>TOURIST

50. MAKE THE MOST OF YOUR TRIP

Wherever you are going, whatever you hope to do we encourage you to embrace it whole-heartedly. Take in the scenery, the culture and above all, enjoy your time away from home.

On a long journey even a straw weighs heavy.

-Spanish Proverb

>TOURIST

PACKING AND PLANNING TIPS

A Week before Leaving

- Arrange for someone to take care of pets and water plants.
- Stop mail and newspaper.
- Notify Credit Card companies where you are going.
- Change your thermostat settings.
- Car inspected, oil is changed, and tires have the correct pressure.
- Passports and photo identification is up to date.
- Pay bills.
- Copy important items and download travel Apps.
- Start collecting small bills for tips.

Right Before Leaving

- Clean out refrigerator.
- Empty garbage cans.
- Lock windows.
- Make sure you have the proper identification with you.
- Bring cash for tips.
- Remember travel documents.
- Lock door behind you.
- Remember wallet.
- Unplug items in house and pack chargers.

>TOURIST

READ OTHER GREATER THAN A TOURIST BOOKS

Greater Than a Tourist San Miguel de Allende Guanajuato Mexico: 50 Travel Tips from a Local by Tom Peterson

Greater Than a Tourist – Lake George Area New York USA: 50 Travel Tips from a Local by Janine Hirschklau

Greater Than a Tourist – Monterey California United States: 50 Travel Tips from a Local by Katie Begley

Greater Than a Tourist – Chanai Crete Greece: 50 Travel Tips from a Local by Dimitra Papagrigoraki

Greater Than a Tourist – The Garden Route Western Cape Province South Africa: 50 Travel Tips from a Local by Li-Anne McGregor van Aardt

Greater Than a Tourist – Sevilla Andalusia Spain: 50 Travel Tips from a Local by Gabi Gazon

Greater Than a Tourist – Kota Bharu Kelantan Malaysia: 50 Travel Tips from a Local by Aditi Shukla

Children's Book: Charlie the Cavalier Travels the World by Lisa Rusczyk

>TOURIST

> TOURIST

Visit Greater Than a Tourist for Free Travel Tips
http://GreaterThanATourist.com

Sign up for the Greater Than a Tourist Newsletter for discount days, new books, and travel information:
http://eepurl.com/cxspyf

Follow us on Facebook for tips, images, and ideas:
https://www.facebook.com/GreaterThanATourist

Follow us on Pinterest for travel tips and ideas:
http://pinterest.com/GreaterThanATourist

Follow us on Instagram for beautiful travel images:
http://Instagram.com/GreaterThanATourist

>TOURIST

> TOURIST

Please leave your honest review of this book on Amazon and Goodreads. Please send your feedback to GreaterThanaTourist@gmail.com as we continue to improve the series. We appreciate your positive and constructive feedback. Thank you.

>TOURIST

METRIC CONVERSIONS

TEMPERATURE

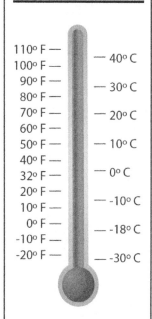

110° F — — 40° C
100° F —
90° F — — 30° C
80° F —
70° F — — 20° C
60° F —
50° F — — 10° C
40° F —
32° F — — 0° C
20° F —
10° F — — -10° C
0° F — — -18° C
-10° F —
-20° F — — -30° C

To convert F to C:

Subtract 32, and then multiply by 5/9 or .5555.

To Convert C to F:
Multiply by 1.8
and then add 32.

32F = 0C

LIQUID VOLUME

To Convert:................Multiply by
U.S. Gallons to Liters................ 3.8
U.S. Liters to Gallons 26
Imperial Gallons to U.S. Gallons 1.2
Imperial Gallons to Liters....... 4.55
Liters to Imperial Gallons 22
1 Liter = .26 U.S. Gallon
1 U.S. Gallon = 3.8 Liters

DISTANCE

To convert ....Multiply by
Inches to Centimeters 2.54
Centimeters to Inches 39
Feet to Meters....................... .3
Meters to Feet 3.28
Yards to Meters 91
Meters to Yards 1.09
Miles to Kilometers 1.61
Kilometers to Miles............ .62
1 Mile = 1.6 km
1 km = .62 Miles

WEIGHT

1 Ounce = .28 Grams
1 Pound = .4555 Kilograms
1 Gram = .04 Ounce
1 Kilogram = 2.2 Pounds

>TOURIST

TRAVEL QUESTIONS

- Do you bring presents home to family or friends after a vacation?

- Do you get motion sick?

- Do you have a favorite billboard?

- Do you know what to do if there is a flat tire?

- Do you like a sun roof open?

- Do you like to eat in the car?

- Do you like to wear sun glasses in the car?

- Do you like toppings on your ice cream?

- Do you use public bathrooms?

- Did you bring your cell phone and does it have power?

- Do you have a form of identification with you?

- Have you ever been pulled over by a cop?

- Have you ever given money to a stranger on a road trip?

- Have you ever taken a road trip with animals?

- Have you ever went on a vacation alone?

- Have you ever run out of gas?

- If you could move to any place in the world, where would it be?
- If you could travel anywhere in the world, where would you travel?
- If you could travel in any vehicle, which one would it be?
- If you had three things to wish for from a magic genie, what would they be?
- If you have a driver's license, how many times did it take you to pass the test?
- What are you the most afraid of on vacation?
- What do you want to get away from the most when you are on vacation?
- What foods smells bad to you?
- What item do you bring on ever trip with you away from home?
- What makes you sleepy?
- What song would you love to hear on the radio when you're cruising on the highway?
- What travel job would you want the least?
- What will you miss most while you are away from home?
- What is something you always wanted to try?

>TOURIST

- What is the best road side attraction that you ever saw?
- What is the farthest distance you ever biked?
- What is the farthest distance you ever walked?
- What is the weirdest thing you needed to buy while on vacation?
- What is your favorite candy?
- What is your favorite color car?
- What is your favorite family vacation?
- What is your favorite food?
- What is your favorite gas station drink or food?
- What is your favorite license plate design?
- What is your favorite restaurant?
- What is your favorite smell?
- What is your favorite song?
- What is your favorite sound that nature makes?
- What is your favorite thing to bring home from a vacation?
- What is your favorite vacation with friends?
- What is your favorite way to relax?

- Where is the farthest place you ever traveled in a car?
- Where is the farthest place you ever went North, South, East and West?
- Where is your favorite place in the world?
- Who is your favorite singer?
- Who taught you how to drive?
- Who will you miss the most while you are away?
- Who if the first person you will contact when you get to your destination?
- Who brought you on your first vacation?
- Who likes to travel the most in your life?
- Would you rather be hot or cold?
- Would you rather drive above, below, or at the speed limited?
- Would you rather drive on a highway or a back road?
- Would you rather go on a train or a boat?
- Would you rather go to the beach or the woods?

>TOURIST

TRAVEL BUCKET LIST

1.

2.

3.

4.

5.

6.

7.

8.

9.

10.

\>TOURIST

NOTES

Made in the USA
Coppell, TX
18 November 2021